THE CO-PARENTING JOURNEY REINVENTED

TEKA DOWNER
FEATURING MARCUS ALLEN

All rights reserved. No portion of this book may be
reproduced in any form without the written permission of the
publisher, Re-Me, llc.

Re-Me Co-Parenting Journey Reinvented

Downer, Teka
Re-Me/Teka Downer, 2019
Copyright © 2019 Teka Downer
ISBN 978-0-578-51707-0
www.icoparent.org

DEDICATION

This book is dedicated to my beautiful son Zion. Your heart and your smile remind me daily that there is an infinite power greater than words could ever express. You represent all that's pure and right with the world, how fortunate am I to be the chosen vessel that gets to mother you. You have been my greatest accomplishment and biggest fan, my life changed forever when your life began.

Love you soooo much ZyBo...love mom.

MY WHY

I have always wanted to write a book explaining the challenges of co-parenting while presenting solutions; however, as I was inspired to write, I felt more led to share my current and past thoughts that promoted inspiration while traveling the co-parenting journey. These thoughts are considered focal points for your consideration during this journey. No two people will have all of the same experiences while co-parenting. Additionally, your experiences may be yours and yours alone, but that does not mean that you cannot peep into the process of those who have found victory on their journey. I hope each page of this motivator both encourages and heals you in ways never known before. May your journey only get better from here.

YOUR WHY

Anytime we make the conscious decision to be better, it's always helpful to have a WHY. Our WHY keeps us motivated, focused and on track with our goals.

Once you have your WHY, post it in a place you can see it daily.

Feel free to journal as we navigate co-parenting together.

_____
_____
_____
_____
_____
_____
_____
_____
_____
_____
_____
_____
_____
_____
_____
_____
_____
_____
_____
_____
_____
_____
_____
_____

STEP 1
PERSPECTIVE

I want this book to inspire, to empower and to heal a community. Co-parenting isn't confined to a certain race, ethnicity, or socio-economic status, but any parent who is no longer in an intimate coexisting relationship with the other parent. Upon the initial acceptance of this journey, one might find his/herself dazed, confused, scared, and a tad hopeful, all in the same moment. But know, that is a moment, and no one moment has the ability to define who you are.

This book would not be complete without diverse perspective. I am a woman who is as stubborn as I am nurturing, I am a realist and yet a bit whimsical. Therefore, my views are shared mainly through those lenses.

I would like to offer some diverse perspective by introducing a key player involved in my co-parenting journey...Marcus, my son's father.

FEAR, FAITH & FORGIVENESS

Growing up, I was always prepared to answer the daunting question of what do you want to be when you grow up. My answer was always the same and stated with confidence "A good dad". The birth of this desire to be a good father came from not having a father in my home. I grew up in a single parent home with a dedicated and determined mother and I promised myself that if given the chance, I would never be a father that was not there for my children. On November 8th, 2007, my dream became a reality with the birth of my son Zion, and in the year of 2011 the fear of not fulfilling my dream of being a great father also became a reality with the divorce from his mother.

FEAR

The next few years fear began to darken the hope I had of being a great dad. How can I be a great dad when I am not in the same home? How will I answer the questions my son will have about why dad is not always there? When will I see my son? The question that haunted me the most was, "Am I going to be just like my dad"? The first step in my co-parenting journey was working through my fear

PERSPECTIVE FROM MARCUS

FAITH

In the midst of working through the fear that had gripped my spirit, I turned to the only gift that sustains when fear darkens your path, faith. My faith in God served as hope for the future and a reminder of my past. God reminded me that every time I faced a challenge, he saw me through my journey. When I was unsure as a twelve-year-old how I would make it to all-star baseball practice, men in my neighborhood stepped up and took me to practice. When I was invited to Augusta State University to visit and accepted a baseball scholarship, my high school baseball coach took me to the visit. When I was in college but did not have a car to get back and forth from class, a guy who ran our team bible study found a car and gave it to me for free. When Zion was born a month early and stayed in the hospital for three weeks, he was cared for by nurses who became angels for our family. When divorce became my reality, my friends provided encouragement, shelter, and hope for my future. Through faith, I learned that everyone needs a village to thrive as a parent and most importantly as a person.

Mutual respect for the co-parent allows the child to see the selflessness needed to be a good parent. My son Zion is blessed that both of his parents have grown and possess the key trait of selflessness.

(2) Remember that we do not own our children, we are only stewards. God is their father and we are responsible for taking care of them. Our children do not need us to be perfect, they have a Heavenly Father who is perfect.

(3) Forgive daily. We must forgive ourselves daily for the mistakes we make as parents. We must forgive the other parent often and remember they are not perfect. As forgiveness provides the freedom to enjoy one of the greatest gifts given to man, our children.

Marcus Allen

STEP 1
PERSPECTIVE
CONTINUED

The first time I read Marcus' words, my heart dropped. Not only are these words from someone that I personally know, but these are words that discuss a past pain that I was partially or partly responsible for. His words allowed me to revisit our past and see him as a genuine human being, dealing with me the best he knew how, given the awful circumstances. His words reminded me of my desire for him to just hurry and adjust to the new world order that I'd put into play. His words reminded me of my selfishness and how some of us on this co-parenting journey, are without grace for the other co-parent, simply because we want a world of our own making. Although my ex and I are in a much better space with co-parenting, his words reminded me that I am still healing, learning, and growing. I was able to peep into his healing process through his words and bare witness that this type of healing was not something that just magically occurred, but it was indeed a process.

A process that looked a whole lot like my own healing process in three steps: Step (1) Perspective. Step (2) Encouragement and Step (3) The Village. This book is formatted by these 3 steps because that is how I recall my healing. First was perspective. When my perspective changed, my life changed. When I began to expect peace instead of the storm, when I learned whatever I put out was returned right back to me, when I learned the value of operating selflessly, my perspective changed. So in turn, my life changed.

Second came encouragement. I learned the authentic power of internal encouragement. This was the encouragement that spoke to my inner doubts and fears with profound authority, even when I willfully wanted to give up. I found encouragement to be my constant and closest companion amid a journey of uncertainty. And third, the village. Changing my perspective and encouraging myself, gave me the strength to be honest with myself and find my people. Or should I say attract my people, my village.

With the first two steps, perspective and encouragement, leading the way of my life, I was more open to living an honest life. I no longer felt the pressure to be what I thought others wanted me to be. I no longer felt I had to have it all together. I was honest to be my broken self and attracted the healers I never knew I needed, my village. I have found that the village will rise when we exist in our most authentic form of our current being, no matter how challenging that may be.

Marcus's perspective is invaluable. Without it, I do not feel this book would be as insightful. My ex-husband and I have been on quite the co-parenting journey, so to share some pages in this book speaks volumes to the power of healing. This type of journey does try your faith, but if you continue the journey you will find your faith tested, then proven.

PERSONAL REFLECTION

Take a moment to consider "your perspective." What role does your perspective play while interacting with your co-parent? Do you need to work on your FAITH? FEAR? FORGIVENESS? Or all three?

STEP 2
ENCOURAGEMENT

"IF WE DO NOT LEARN HOW TO CO-PARENT EFFECTIVELY, THE CHILD SUFFERS."

The other day, I overheard a conversation between a man and a woman discussing their future together. Then all of a sudden, the man comes to a halt and says, "You know what, we can't continue this relationship. My child's mother is just going to make life hell for us." I whipped around so fast, as if I were the woman in that conversation. I saw the woman with tears in her eyes, shaking her head in disbelief, and the man was a bit misty-eyed as well. My food was up, so I left the corner of that painful conversation, walked to my car, and cried. I cried for the woman because I felt her pain. I cried for the man because I could understand his dilemma. I cried for the mother of his child, because I could only imagine her anger towards him was due to unresolved pain. But I cried most for that child. In that moment, I realized that child was being reared by parents who had yet to find a sustainable path to co-parenting and would limit their lives and limit their happiness due to conflict. I realized that both would live in dysfunction and call it life, simply because they had yet to reach that grand pinnacle of conflict resolution.

If we do not learn how to co-parent effectively, the child suffers. If we do not learn how to co-parent effectively, we suffer.

Co-parenting is a challenge, <u>not a death sentence</u>. You are still allowed to live your life.

[14]

FOCAL POINT

"TO THINE OWN SELF BE TRUE."
– Polonius, Hamlet - William Shakespeare

In this very moment, be real with yourself. No one ever said the journey of being a co-parent would be easy; however, it will be worth it! It is completely okay to do an honest assessment of where you are in this moment of your life. If you are happy, say so. If you are confused and angry, say so. If you are a bit numb and not sure what to do, say so. There is a lot to be said for our healing, and self-sustainability, when we are honest with ourselves.

2 ENCOURAGEMENT

WE MASTER THE ART OF CO-PARENTING WHEN WE ARE MINDFUL OF THE ADULTS OUR CHILDREN WILL BECOME

As much as we feel this is about us, and how we feel, it is our duty, our obligation, to make sure we give our children the best tools today, to be productive adults tomorrow.

SOME MOMENTS OF THIS JOURNEY WILL LEAVE YOU FEELING...

like a human see-saw. As soon as you are up, some opposing force sneaks in with the ability to pull you down. Stay mindful. These moments will come and go, but never forget the seesaw has this amazing ability to find balance...and so do you.

IT'S OKAY TO BE AVAILABLE

Some unresolved issues may cause you to pull away from the co-parent or even become distant. But remember, this is the person helping you to rear this amazing human being, so if you can be there for the co-parent, be there. If you can help pick up your kid when the co-parent is running late, be there. It is more than okay to be available.

COMMUNICATE EVEN IF IT'S HARD ...

There will be moments when communicating with the co-parent may feel impossible, communicate anyway. Lack of communication is the foundation upon which unresolved issues are built on.

DISAGREEMENTS ARE TEMPORARY

As are the emotions that are attached to the disagreement. Although in the moment, they don't feel like it.

FORGIVENESS

Intentionally operate from the perspective of forgiveness instead of resentment. When operating from this perspective, benefits are received on both your end and your co-parent. In most circumstances, you have the power to dictate the type of parenting environment you wish to live in, with a few belief adjustments. It will be challenging to operate from the perspective of forgiveness but take the challenge, and not the comfort of living in offense. Offense leads to resentment.

SETTLE ISSUES QUICKLY

Don't allow unresolved issues to remain unresolved for long periods of time. Identify the issue you may be having with your co-parent, then address the issue with your co-parent. When addressing issues, use care and compassion, and put yourself in the other person's shoes.

From time to time,
emotions can
cloud judgment
and cloudy judgment can
lead to a lifetime
of regret.

CO-PARENTING IS ABOUT THE BALANCE OF GRACE EXPRESSED AND GRACE RECEIVED.

It is certainly true that you reap what you sow. If you sow kindness, you MUST expect to receive kindness. Likewise, with your co-parent, if you are busy extending grace, don't forget to expect grace.

FIND THE STRENGTH TO HAVE THE BIG CONVERSATION...

It has been said, that you will either pay on the front end or the back end, the choice is yours. If you run from the challenging conversations that need to be had with your co-parent, then you are doing yourself and your child more harm than good.

IN LIFE

Some things work out perfectly while others are a total bust. The biggest lesson to learn from your mistakes, is to LEARN from your mistakes.

WHEN YOU ARE THE ONLY ONE TRYING

What do you do when you are the only one trying? You keep trying. You keep trying because your child is worth every try you have available. You find someone who you love and trust, and you trust them with the efforts you are making. Just because the co-parent doesn't see or value your effort, doesn't mean your efforts have to go unnoticed.

CHOOSE PEACE!

Of course life will have its way of presenting difficult situations, even on the best of days, but you still have a choice in the matter. You can choose to go with the difficulties, or you can choose peace. Let that choice be a tool in your toolbox of co-parenting. It will serve you well.

> "YOU CAN CHOOSE TO GO WITH THE DIFFICULTIES, OR YOU CAN CHOOSE PEACE."

ENCOURAGEMENT

IS IT ME...?

Or does this journey feel impossible? Unless an amazing agreement was established from the beginning with you and the co-parent, there will be times when you feel as if storms of life are the norm. But they aren't. This journey will have its peaks and its valley moments, but stay encouraged in knowing, no storm can last forever. Eventually the rain stops pouring, the clouds clear away, and the sun shines effortlessly.

IT'S A JOURNEY NOT A TRIP

Typically, we are given a heads up before we begin any journey, so therefore we know how to prepare. This particular journey, however, gives no true heads up, so we must prepare along the way and that is ok. Just know, this is not a quick trip and it will require marathon type stamina.

ALL ISN'T LOST...

do not think for one moment that you have ruined your life or your child's life. Challenges of life will find us all from time to time. Your job is to keep traveling, and eventually even ground will appear.

IF YOU CAN GO THROUGH IT, AND IT DOES NOT KILL YOU...

that simply means it has the potential to make you stronger. There will be many situations on this journey that feel impossible. Stay encouraged and stay hopeful, because there is a big difference between something feeling impossible versus it actually being impossible.

ENCOURAGEMENT

EVERY PRISON ISN'T PHYSICAL...

There are times we lock ourselves up in psychological prisons that can do more harm than any physical prison ever could. Do not become a prisoner of your thoughts.

DON'T REST IN YOUR FEAR

If you find yourself being afraid of this process, you're not the only one. This entire journey is frightening, because sometimes it's hard to see the next step; however, you owe it to yourself not to stay in that fear. Fear will paralyze you and then consume your life. Confront every fear with your beautiful truth.

FOCAL POINT | AFFIRM THIS WITH ME:

My life unfolds beautifully as it is supposed to and today is no exception.

Affirmations are powerful, do not be afraid to affirm positivity over your life.

PERSONAL REFLECTION

At this moment, take some time to think about your village. What does your village look like? How do you feel about adding new people who are beneficial or exiting old people who no longer add value?

STEP 3: THE VILLAGE

In the introduction of this book, my ex-husband spoke candidly about his fear. His fear of not being a good father to our son Zion due to us no longer being in the traditional home setting. His writing reminded me of the disagreements that we dealt with when newly divorced. Looking back, I can see our disagreements were fueled with our individual fears. Of course, there were other things that caused tension, but fear was the foundation of our arguments. I was afraid that every day of my life would be an argument with my ex about our child or at least until Zion was an adult. That fear often tricked me, because it presented something that wasn't true.

I've often heard fear stood for false evidence appearing to be real, and that became my new found truth. Both my ex and I were allowing false evidence to create our realities. We were being driven by our fears not our truth. Although my ex isn't much older than me, I often credit him for teaching me some valuable life lessons. One being "make a decision based off of truth not emotion." At some point in our journey, I decided to stand on the truth of my being and not the emotion of my circumstance.

When he would present his fears, I would tell him the truth.
When I would present my fears to myself, asking questions if I was doing the right thing or being led by emotion, I would present myself with my truth.

It is apparent that once we both overcame our fears, we were able to reestablish the village that our son needed.

And that has made all the difference...

DO SOMETHING THAT SHOCKS YOU, AS IT PERTAINS TO YOUR CO-PARENT

How about pay a compliment from time to time to the one who is helping you rear another human being? Shocking, I know! But sometimes it is necessary. You never know the secret parenting battles the other parent may be facing. A parenting compliment may be all that is needed to overcome a daily challenge.

DON'T GIVE UP ON YOU...

If you find yourself being afraid of this process, you're not the only one. This entire journey is frightening, because sometimes it's hard to see the next step; however, you owe it to yourself not to stay in that fear. Fear will paralyze you and then consume your life. Confront every fear with your beautiful truth.

Remember that your hopes and dreams are still a real thing. I know it is easy to allow this to distract, or even depress you, but it is a **MUST** that you not give up on you. Recall your dreams. Set new goals you can still achieve. Your child will appreciate you going for your goals, because a more fulfilled parent can raise a more fulfilled child.

IT'S OK TO HAVE A GOOD DAY

This journey has peaks and lows. And for whatever reason, you may think you deserve to live in the valley lows. That could not be further from the truth. You are a human being and you are dealing with some results of your human choices. It is totally ok for you to have a good day. Do not allow guilt to be your constant companion. It is more than ok to travel with goodness from time to time.

YOU ARE NOT ALONE

There will be moments when you feel you are in this by yourself. There will be moments when it all feels hopeless and effort is worthless, but these are just moments. Don't allow the emotion of a moment, to make you feel, as if this is your permanent destination. You are not alone. You are not without a tribe who does not understand you. During this journey, I have found it comforting to speak with others who have found the successful path to co-parenting. Identify your tribe and fight the emotion of feeling alone.

REMEMBER...

That situation that you thought was going to be the death of you? You know the situation that kept you from getting rest at night, consumed all your thoughts, drained you of your energy? Yea that situation, which took some time to get over, but you OVERCAME it. You found a strength you never knew you had because of that situation. You learned a lesson you never knew you needed because of that situation. Likewise, with co-parenting, this journey contains valuable jewels worth collecting.

YOU ARE GRACED

To get through this. If for whatever reason you find yourself in such an unbelievable situation, know in this moment, you have grace to get through it. It took me a minute to learn this lesson, but I have finally learned it. If you are in it, there is grace readily available to sustain you through it.

THIS PROCESS

Will one day, birth a version of you, that you will love. I recall growing thru one of the darkest chapters of my life and reading a quote that said; "one day you will greet yourself with a smile and no longer know the stranger of sadness you appear to be." I read it, but couldn't quiet grasp it. The words were clear, but the emotional pain overwhelmed my comprehension; however, I never let those words go. I remember the day I was able to smile at myself as the sadness was leaving and the lesson was being learned. You too, will one day find, that this journey birthed a more beautiful, polished, wiser, healthier, evolved version of you.

THIS MIGHT SURPRISE YOU

But what others think of you has nothing to do with you. During this process you might wonder and worry about what others are thinking of you. You may become consumed, thinking about what the friends and families of your co-parent think of you. That is normal and human nature, but you mustn't let it consume you. You would fare well to confront why you are worried about what others think of you. Once you have confronted your worry, revisit your truth and rest in that place.

THERE IS ONLY ONE YOU!

It is normal to wrestle with the thoughts of another person taking your place in your child's life. You are not the first person to have these thoughts, nor will you be the last. But rest assured, no one can take your place in your child's life. As convincing as those lies are, do not come into agreement with those thoughts.

BLENDED FAMILY OR BLENDED

I had a brilliant conversation the other day with a step-mom who joked about the idea of what it meant to be a blended family. She jokingly said, "Blended? More like thrown together, chopped up, broken into a million pieces, then marred together!" I had the best laugh from her statement -because I can recall a time feeling exactly what she was describing. When thinking of a blended family, a nice picture comes to mind. But the reality of achieving the perfect blend can be very challenging. Smoothies are great, they taste amazing, but without the blending process we are stuck with bland chunks.

BE YOUR OWN ADVOCATE

You have every God given right in the world to be the best mother or father that you can be. Don't allow your "right now" circumstance to dictate how you parent. Increase your self-talk, tell yourself you are amazing, and you only get more amazing with each passing day. Advocate for your rights to be your child's parent, believe you were divinely called to be your child's parent, advocate for you.

YOU ARE WELL EQUIPPED FOR THIS JOURNEY...

Even if it doesn't feel like it. A popular therapist who I listen to often, constantly says "feelings are without an IQ." They have no intelligence level whatsoever. That is why they are so easily swayed. Stop believing what it feels like and trust that you are well equipped for any obstacle that comes your way.

WHY KEEP GOING?

Keep going because one day you will see the fruit of your labor. One day you will look up and realize what once challenged you, no longer bothers you. Keep going because one day your child will grow into an incredible adult (and you not having quit,) will have a great deal to do with it.

OBSTACLES

Are going to exist for our children whether we like it or not. Let's not add unnecessary obstacles, by not effectively co-parenting...

REST EASY

Each night by way of quiet reflection. Reflect on your day. Did you do well in the co-parenting arena? Great. If you didn't do so well, that is still ok. If you are blessed with a new day, just know, another day means another chance.

IT TAKES A VILLAGE

To raise a completed child, it will take more than just you. It is going to take you, your child's other parent, ideally, your new partner and the other parent's partner; perhaps some grands, a few aunts and uncles, some good teachers, coaches, wise spiritual leaders, and a whole host of others. It truly takes a village! Do not try to go it alone, the world is filled with learning experiences and there is no way you can expose your child to all of them single handedly.

This journey will be continual and has the ability to mature you in ways you've never known. Whether you are with the child's other parent or not, parenting has the ability to make you an avid student of life.

The reinvention of co-parenting has birthed a village of people who choose to display how committed they are to co-parenting. The name of our village is i-coparent. Our name answers the question, if you are no longer with your child's mother/father, how are you raising your child...our collective response, i-coparent.

We are here to help and support one another, we are here to restore broken-parent relationships too. If you would like more helpful hints on co-parenting, please go to www.icoparent.org and subscribe to our site.

PERSONAL REFLECTION

NEXT STEPS

Clearly you can see this wasn't a tough read or a long one for that matter. So now is the part where you add your steps. List your next steps for improving your co-parenting journey. Revisit these steps, revisit this book, and develop more steps.

NOTES

www.ingramcontent.com/pod-product-compliance
Lightning Source LLC
Chambersburg PA
CBHW071241090426
42736CB00014B/3171